THE TAPESTRY IN QUESTION

For
our children

CONTENTS

First

First, the shimmering lights.
And last, an intimate reluctant
  farewell, fleeing ahead of
  dawn's breaking.
Venturing from a hesitant
  planning of its itinerary,
time lustfully raced,
  savored and shared
  by the greed of innocence.
A crescendo and cacophony
  of pleasures,
the night was a wonderful
  presentation.

Sand Castle (Version II)

Constructed near water's edge,
to assure the use of the best materials,
the castle
(like all those built before it
on this beach, since before
castles were known to exist)
stood as a sentinel guard
protecting the innocence and joy
and spirit of passion
from which
its walls
and turrets
and passageways
and moat—lurking with
scuzzy muck within its basin—
were assembled
and artfully adorned
with carefully collected
selections from the
surrounding debris of the sea.
But as sun's heat
dries the sand,
and winds gently swirl away
the walls
and turrets
and passageways,

while waves
(against which the moat
provides no defense)
persistently lap
and slap
at the foundations,
melt away into but another
gentle hill
which had been built so well,
so noble—briefly—in its aspirations,
where shall we find
new protections
for the fragile creatures
of joy,
innocence
and passion
now left unguarded
against the inexorable
eroding forces
of reality
and time?

Night Dreams

So mindful is the night
of the secrets of our dreams.
How rich the tales,
both histories and fantasies,
to which we turn
our thoughts
with the passing
of the children's hour.
More often than
we admit,
dawn's light is but
the fading of our vision
of the most fulfilling
moments of the day.
Inexorable are
the routines of living,
how comforting
and exhilarating
can be our retreat
into the sanctuary
of the darkness.

Dream with my dreams,
allow me to share
your tales.
Night after night,
let us find
and feast together
upon the riches
of the darkness,
and there satiate
our appetite for life.

Despair

Despair numbs me
sedating
the protests of my soul—
anguished cries
against inexorable pain,
silent—
corroding
through the night
leaving bared
only
the lack of courage,
a fatal, unkempt boil
upon my heart.

Tomorrow

Tomorrow
while still wrapped
in the comforting discretion
of waning night,
as you rest, peaceful
but not yet awake,
I shall wish to love you,
love you slowly as I have yet to do.

Tomorrow
I shall wish to create
and to feast upon our love,
not with rampaging passion
but with deliberate,
unmeasured pace,
a pace to which one
only rarely slows,
a pace reserved to savor
those few precious moments
when true beauty confronts,
arouses and caresses the soul.

Tomorrow,
ahead of dawn's light,
I shall wish to cherish you,
allowing,
even before I first touch,

the fragrances
of your hair, your skin
your sex
to drift
to mingle and be inhaled,
a seductive bouquet upon which
to intoxicate myself
and be drawn beyond
conventions and patterns
of past intercourses
into a new, exquisitely detailed
unfolding collage
of delicacies,
emotions
and indrawn breaths.

No more quickly
than beads of dew
form and wash
a leaf of yesterday's dust
shall I wish to first
stroke and warm
your face,
fingers extending
to explore and
understand
each detail, each mark
of character
upon your face,
your limbs, your chest,

moving as lightly
across
around, under
within
as morning mist
might float above
a hidden, secret
forest pond.

Tomorrow,
I shall wish to kiss you
gently, completely
as a doe might welcome
her fawn into life,
intimately cleansing
away the residue
of all which preceded
our love, leaving you
cherished, warmed
and innocent,
sheltered from the world
by my caresses and embrace.

And, as tomorrow nears,
as this day's light succumbs
to night and poetry's cathartic
power fades,
I shall wish nothing more
but that wishes
can come true.

Parking Lot

There,
do you hear her approaching step?
Beyond the mesh wire
that reaches
about the lot—rusting screens
holding out
the prying eyes
of those not really wanting
to see within.

Crouch here
behind the wall.
From this spot,
her arrival is most
easily observed.
Most nights
she is the last to leave,
the lot empty of all
but two cars that remain
each week
from Monday till Friday.

Is the snow that falls,
leaving puddles in her path,
but frozen tears of apathy,
warmed to wetness by the heat
of our passion
for the violence
soon to come?

The snow's silence
will absorb her screams.
Time it
so the only sound will be
the rattle of the subway
above us.

Now . . .

Anniversary

Each day is filled
with my thoughts of you.
Each dawn my heart breaks,
    as I leave you
    or realize, apart,
    that I have left you
    to rise alone.
Each night
my mind turns to you,
the day complete
if I can but touch—
flesh to flesh—
and link together
while you slumber
two spirits meant
to live as one.
Each year passes
more quickly,
my hunger for you
more demanding,
my appetite
less often satiated.
Let us continue
to travel together,
each day a life itself,
continuing to seek
fulfillment
of our uncommon love.

Morning Soliloquy

That I might be
this morn with thee
disturbing your serenity
not from afar
but from little further
than the distance
between my lips
and thine ear,
as I whisper quietly
so that none could hear
save you
the sweet and delicious
melody
of simple words of love—
bites of ripened fruits,
fresh with frosty dew
served gently
with insatiable affection
as this day's first repast.

That I might share
this morn's bright glare,
a glorious enlightening
of the passions
of the day to come,
embraced not by the solitude
in this my sterile chamber,
high above the chaos
of a city awakening,
but held tight
against your flesh,
flushed and breathless
from yet earlier excursions,
stretched across

a rumpled set of linen
in a room vibrant and afire,
not with nature's illumination
but with tokens and mementos
of other dawns
other nights
and other passions.

That I might conclude
and bring to a close
this oft-excruciating prelude.
The accelerating crescendo
of emotions,
developed well
from happenstance,
rests unfinished,
awaiting the substance
of the tale to yet be scribed
across the blank crisp pages
of the folio
which lies open upon our hearts.

With these thoughts
my mind is occupied
in this the darkness
before the dawn.
Slumber long forsaken
as my heart, my body,
my soul
are drawn
to consciousness
by the frustration
by the solitude
by the passions . . .

First Impressions

Misplaced pennies found in the haystack
    downpayments for thoughts remaining unspoken.
Her feet idle now, bearing grudges against the absence
    of apparent suicides just beyond the fingertips.
Masking affection for life's dances,
    her humor corrodes; once pounding rhythms
    (known to all, but undefinable)
    rendered repetitious and unappealing.
Not provoked from more than the heart,
    her lust for the uncertainty of adventure
    retires,
    satisfied by silvery images of the shadowed past.
Chilled swirls of bourbon holding favor
    over mother's milk
    for the half-orphaned child.

Flight of Fancy

High above pillowing clouds,
slipping across miles
of earth below,
I can think of but
one small raspberry,
ripe and succulent,
poised as the last of
a fine line of raspberries
recently devoured
while traipsing carelessly
down a path from the nape of your neck,
down,
down your spine's curve,
resting now alone,
waiting as the last
to be caressed and embraced
by my lips,
leaving behind but one drop
of its nectar,
to be slowly savored
upon my tongue
as but a flavoring
of the seemingly endless
offerings
of the seemingly endless
nights of our love.

Carousel

She arrived,
a solitary guest in the garden,
far earlier than required.
Her steps
the only tampering
of the last winter snow,
fallen unexpectedly
from the darkness
of the night just departed.
Now tucked
within the shadows
of aged, white-dusted pines
that towered
beyond eastern fence,
shadows thick
but honed sharp
by morning sun,
rising into cloudless sky,
the bench
was still the proper place—
brushed clean at one end—
from which she could contemplate
the scheduled rendezvous
and the lazy stretching
of the awakening day,
an aged, proper coat not quite enough
to insulate

against a shiver
both from shadow's chill
   and from within,
a reflex
to keep in check anxiety
— that in his heart
   the passion,
   still held in her heart
   for him,
   might be now devoted
   to another
— that time, distance
   or other inconveniences
   which masquerade
   as justifiable excuses
   might yet outweigh
   his good intentions
   to return
— that her relinquishment
   of responsibility
   to honor his oath, long ago
   breathlessly given
   with last embrace,
   was but a foolish escapade—
   an adventure without substance
   which would not release her
   from confinement
   within the routines of living

— that, for any reason,
    the promise made
    might pass, on this the appointed day,
    unkept
— that, despite all reason,
    the promise made
    might, on this the appointed day,
    be upheld.

So carefully constructed
in the rituals of autumn
to protect,
the casing about the carousel
now awaited dismantling
as the opening episode
in the rituals of the spring.
She sat witness
as workers worked,
wielding crowbars and hammers
and bad dispositions,
their breaths, exhaled,
still frozen by the near-still air,
drawing her attention
from tightenings within.
Quiet broken
by the squeaks of nails
protesting
their extraction—

Assembled, grayed panels
again disassembled,
stacked to the side,
releasing back to the garden
the animals within
— well-shaped steeds
   in perpetual good form
— nostrils flaring
   beneath painted bridles
— heads tossed strongly
   against the wind,
   ever blowing
   from the front
— flanks flexed and muscled
— hooves poised to gallop,
   but forever silent,
   suspended inches above asphalt turf
   beneath gilded saddles.

Here, she recalled,
on this bench they had shared,
together with the horses,
the goings and comings
of one summer night's attendance,

a menagerie
of all those attracted
— by streaming,
   blinking lights
— by ageless, discordant
   melodies
— by joyful smiles
   and occasional cries
   (some of laughter
   and some of tears)
   brought by the breezes
   from the circling, speeding
   stampede.

A repeating illusion
of escapes.
of fantasies.
of dreams.
A vibrant, blurring
wild cacophony—
like their love
she reminisced.

Now—
as the shadows retreated
as the snow melted away,
as the final morning hour passed—
left by the workmen
(departing
from a job
quickly finished),

the carousel stood ready
to continue in its melodies
— a promised destination
— a landmark
    for dreams coming true
— a companion
    to the lady on the bench,
waiting again
on this first day of spring.

Conference Room

Paling, breathing corpses
lit by the glow
of fluorescent gases
rather than warming rays
of June's first summer sun,
banging heads
in existentialistic rhythms
against windowless walls
of steel catacombs
from which financial nectars
are harvested
by those already too rich
to appreciate the smile
which a second cold soda
on a hot summer day
can bring to the ghetto child
of the absent mother
who silently serves
to the corpses
excessive quantities
of rye bread sandwiches.
A materially adverse non-existence.

Untitled

O, how full the moon tonight
the sky cloudless
as two fortnights past,
when still air—
moving not leaves
nor rippling waters—
was filled
with the near fluorescent
reflections
of earlier passions of the day
and exhaustion
failed to contain
yet further entanglements
and explorations
beneath the moon.

On the Occasion of Lunch

On this unusual November day,
despite
the crashing forces
of structural reconstructions
abounding
and
brutal buffetings
of a lost spring wind
(stripping away
the last few leaves
of a summer full of life),
the delicate
fragile framework
of a lasting friendship
— reinforced
   by but a bit
   of unabashed, gentle and
   mutual affection—
endured,
reaffirming the strength
of the genuine passions
with which the world
and life
are to be embraced.

Return Journey

The portals to the world
remain as they were.
Chaotic noise—
a Babel spread
from gate to gate
moving in shuffled steps
and hurried hustling—
no different
than the time before.
Welled in my heart
an impression,
but a step or two
into the fray,
a mood rising,
moistened by
unchecked tears,
of emptiness
and solitude,
for now I travelled—
again repeating
our journey—
unaccompanied by the cadence
of your heart,
silent to all but my heart.

For now I waited
in one line, then another,
without the camaraderie
of affectionate glances
shared,
appearing to others
as that which we were,
intimate companions
journeying
toward a destination
uncharted except within our souls.

For now I went alone,
melodies of love songs
just recently played
the only harmonies
in my mind
for the rapturous memories
of our travels
before.

Untitled

Now I know how
she feels.
When I work late
when I travel
when I bring the
  bullshit home.
Now I know
how it feels
to be second
and left to the side
more often than not.
Now I know
the hurt
of that which is honest
and real
being hidden beneath,
denied to enhance
self-preservation
in a world
of that which is unreal.
Now I know
how she feels.

Fragments

Fragments of thoughts.
Interrupted illusions.
We struggle to carve
with our own idle words
the small bits of our souls
which we have the courage
   to know.
Hastily (time passes so quickly),
we stumble over each other
to reveal but those portions
of our selves
that may be disposed of
in the trash
of adult conversation.

Frustrated by the inadequacy
   of our words
to complete the fragments
and thereby portray
the dimensions we have not
the daring to discover,
we may, and do, indulge
in the convenience of what
society tolerates, that being
intercourse which is
other than social.

Nude, but not naked,
essences draped by the ripples
of an exterior veneer
that sweat has produced
and which only mirrors
truly appreciate.

The realities of which
we are constructed,
and not the illusions,
are within, inconvenient.
Chipped and worn by our
    persistent self-sculpting,
they are perhaps only visible
when discovered by others.

Eye to eye with another,
over time and without haste,
I yearn—
    to discover and to be exposed.
    to be languorously entwined,
    sensually caressing the soul.
    to cling passionately
    with the pain, and the pleasure.
    to recline, while surrounded
    by the lingering musky
    aromas
    of completed realities.

Halloween

Tonight,
amidst goblins and ghouls
whose screams are
hardly terrifying,
while leisurely kicking aside
the skeletal, crinkling
remains
of late summer's lushness,
strolling beneath
a sky of unsettling
blackness,
I discovered
a more horrific
nightmare than either
Hallmark or
Hollywood might conceive.
Within my heart,
disturbingly close
to the essence
of my soul,
lurking behind the daily
illusions with which
we nourish
our fragile, mutual affections,
was the specter
of solitude.

Summer Moon

Rising moon,
full through evening fog
and heavy in the lingering heat
of the day's summer bake,
illuminates this anniversary
of other nights, other dreams.
Few wounds upon the heart
heal with time—
like trees ravaged
by men's carvings of summer loves,
we too grow around the wounds,
growing older, but remaining
injured until life escapes.
On this well-lit night,
beneath familiar moon
(recurring witness to
other dreams, including other
dreams coming true),
how I again can only dream
that the wounds left
by dreams left behind—
and the persistent pain
which stays on—
might be healed
by the light
of tomorrow's moon.

Wisteria

Beneath heavy, aged vines
laced with fragrant blooms
of spring's passions,
my caresses shall unsheath
thy soul,
slowly, tenderly
exposing your heart
to the arousing spirits
which dance upon the wind
and drift—
drift silently
into this private garden—
to join me
in embracing you
through the night
until dawn's glow
is reflected from
your cheeks,
still moistened
by fallen tears,
as you rest
in satiated slumber
within my arms.

The Tapestry in Question

From fragmentary scraps
fallen to the floor,
forgotten tatterings
overlooked
in favor of
crisp, virgin cloth,
she suggested
the most passionate tapestries
may be woven.

Recovered from the floor,
brushed of dirt and dust balls
and stretched taut
to smooth
the wrinkles and crinkles
acquired in the heaping
of other discarded remnants,
certain clippings yet held
the subtle elegance,
the special hues,
not first seen
when cleanly rolled,
unmeasured and uncut,
in uniform bolts.

The seamstress—
herself left behind
by time's passage,
shoulders bent by years
of inadequate
light,
fingertips smoothed
by miles and miles
of patterned garments
fed "by the piece"
through whirring needles,
but eyes still clear,
sharp enough to guide
her search—
the seamstress sought
the proper collection
with knowing sureness,
finding in the excess and waste
of earlier projects
the necessary elements
to complete a weaving
satisfactory
to my exacting
specifications.

For, having wandered
inadvertently into
the maze
of congested by-passes
and detours,

ancient
but still seductive
in their attractiveness,
that clogged the space
between
the structured thoroughfares
on which commerce
now flowed,
I had unexpectedly
found
across dusty sill
and through open door,
grayed paint
flaked by neglect,
a passage
to the end of
my search
for an adequate recollection
and
appropriate remembrance.

And so it was
that she wove my tapestry,
and found the special threads

to illustrate—until,
long past our deaths,
the stitches decay away
leaving
but cleaning rags
for our children's
children—
to illustrate and display
in brilliant intimacy
that which I had asked
to be portrayed
— fingers curling
    amidst soft swirls
    of hair
— the wetness
    of a well-nibbled ear,
    cooled by the soft breeze
    of a circling fan
— the pressing weight
    of hip bones
    against the quiet direction
    of outstretched
    calloused palms
— whimpered pleasures
    spoken by lips
    otherwise distracted

— neck tendons,
   tensed and thick,
   inadequately resisting
   impulsive reactions
   to feathery strokes
   across delicate parts
— hands laced
   in mock combat—
   a horizontal
   battle pose above
   betrayed
   by parting thighs
   below
— sheets crumpled,
   piled by footwork
   climbing toward
   expectations
— dawn's light
   upon an exposed souvenir,
   a fading arch
   of passion bitten.

Such is the tale
of the tapestry
of which you have inquired.

Je t'aime

Je t'aime.
In the solitude
of this room,
scattered with
the disordered remains
of unsuccessful diversions
and defenses
against the loneliness
and the quiet—
the quiet which seeps
into this austere cubicle
through the cracked
panes of smog-rotted glass
from the abandoned courtyard
below upon which I stare,
filled only with refuse,
discarded chairs,
moist green moss
and a wayward cat—
here my soul finds rest
tonight,
and my mind remains sane,
only because
je t'aime.

The Rose

Soft as woven, warm silk,
edged in the crimson color of lust unrestrained,
each yellow petal—plucked—
floats tenderly to rest,
weightless,
a blanket tucking beneath
the moist, lingering heat of a languorous kiss.
One hundred coverings for
    one hundred adorations,
singular, melodic notes laying across
the folio of her rising, falling chest,
harmonizing to the symphonic crescendo
of accelerating pulses
that shape into sound
but one breathless word—
"more".

Darkness

Always alone at the end
of the night,
left awake, staring at
your resting countenance,
I am companioned
only by my insecurities
and nightmares—
demons who reside
behind the illumination
of the day.
Always alone at the end
of the night,
never tucked to sleep
despite my exhaustion.
Always alone
in the aching solitude
of the darkness.

Liaison on the Beach

Not alone, yet solitary.
The trail of naked feet
from lapping, receding tide
the only disruption
of the wide, volcanic beach
which you claimed to yourself.
From beyond the gentle curls
of early morning waves,
adrift
between the heat
of rising sun
and the inviting crescent
of the shore,
I was distracted
not by your presence,
but by the assertive confidence
with which you had occupied
the sand.

Not merely an idle visitor,
to be timidly confined
within
a cloth square
spread evenly and perpendicular
to the surf,
you had chosen instead
to lay directly upon the earth,
unclothed,

spread fully to absorb
the warmth of the day's arrival,
with well-worn grains
of ancient mountain rock
lightly veiling
the underside of your flesh.

To your left, a woven basket
with the remains
of a fruitful repast before it,
accompanied (in disregard
of proper morning etiquette)
by a bottle of champagne,
well consumed.
And, to your right,
carefully laid face down,
just beyond your fingertips,
a book, lacking the attraction
to divert your concentration
from the basking of the sun.

Missing from this private tableau,
disconcerting as omissions,
were discarded garments
and, perhaps more puzzling,
any trace of passage
from the forest's edge.
No soft paddings
across the beach—
no careless, joyful
kicks of celebration—

only your steps from the water
as testimony
to your origin—
no hints as to
your later destination.

Brought closer,
drawn by the rhythmic massage
of the moon's pull
beneath the rough-hewn boards
of the discarded skiff
I had claimed from the shore
under night's cloak
(in which, in an intoxicated state
some hours before, I had believed
whales could be searched
and discovered),
I float just yards away,
near scraping against
the patterned sand waves below,
as all that you are
now becomes more visible.

Motionless,
save for the soft swell of your chest,
rising and falling obligingly
to capture life's breath,
and for the fluid beads
of sweat, glistening
as they fall across
downward curves,

yours was a pose
from an imaginary tale come true,
an embracement
with full passion
of elegant fantasy,
nudity framed
by nature and man's
finer contributions.

Stepping now across the beach,
I see no flinch
of outstretched limbs,
eyes remaining closed
to my approach,
forehead still moistening
in defense against
the warming day.
Now a part of your
well-planned tableau,
I crouch beside you,
and as my shadow
lays across your eyes,
your lips belie the presence
of experience,
forming, so gently,
the smile of a woman
who has anticipated,
who has emerged, and
who has savored with expectation
the seduction of this dawn.

And, as I bend
to first kiss from your brow
the salty dew,
and then to caress
with my fingers
and my lips
all which the sun and the sand,
at your beckoning,
have embraced,
the sea breeze
brings to me
your musky aroma,
your invitation to be your guest
in a passionate liaison
on the beach.

Untitled

As the edge of dawn
still crawls
toward the eastern shore,
night's darkness
embracing you in quiet, peaceful slumber,
I awake—
seized by the rolling,
throbbing pulse of love
pounding
through my head,
my heart—
inner soul consumed
by a frenetic rhythm—
that of an untamed herd
of spring stallions
galloping across an unfenced,
virgin field
in a race with the morning sun,
unshod hooves
caressing dew-laced turf
in unorchestrated, chaotic
thundering percussion.

Such is the rhythm
by which now must I pace
the moments
awaiting
dawn's light,
your kiss upon my waiting lips
and the arrival
of the gut-wrenching pain
with which I must endure
once again
farewell.

Her Hat

Her hat sits
above the clutter of
everyday chaos
which litters
the floor, the bed
and the dresser top—
remnants of morning indecisions
and evening exhaustions—
resting in a position
of prominence
so that it not be
confused amongst
the other trappings
and adornments,
both practical
and not-so
with which
daily outfits
are assembled
and the bedroom
redecorated.
First placed after
perhaps too much
deliberation but
with a quiet smile

(recalling to mind
the manner in which
hats, caps and chapeaus—
when worn correctly—
serve not to cover
nor protect, but
to draw from within
the essence of that
which is real
and to dress the spirit
with authentic vestments),
the hat's colors remain genuine,
despite the fine, thin dust
which adorns its brim—
proof conclusive that
worn but once, the hat
has since remained
unworn,
serving only to remind her,
on occasion and in passing,
that good housekeeping
should more often reach
above waist level—
and its shape remains
true.

For unlike a good hat—
a real hat—
its not been
tossed, grabbed,
crushed, blown,
recovered, misplaced,
rediscovered
or cleaned.
No, this accessory
of fashion, though
idle, serves still its original
purpose and continues
to seduce her from
within its fibres, its
lining and its stitches.
And waits,
with patience,
confident that it
shall yet be worn—
worn like a real hat
discharging its function as
an accoutrement of
significance, revealing:
— the warm, full openness
    with which she welcomes the world
— the calm, sweet grace
    harvested
    from satisfying explorations
    in the past

— the slightly mischievous
smile, anticipating
future excursions, and
— the childlike pout
of a woman never grown.
For just once,
since first laid to rest
(intended to be inconspicuous, but
provided a place of honor,
nonetheless,
as earlier described),
on a late Sunday morn,
after the daily rituals
had subsided
and the rooms of the house
had been evacuated of all but her
by the callings
of others' commitments,
before the dresser mirror
naked, patted dry
from the shower
but still wet within
the creases and folds of
her flesh,
she returned, in the
solitude of the moment
(her pose
unfamiliar amidst
the normalcy from which
the hat had been
so carefully isolated),

she returned
to the feelings,
the emotions and
the recollections of
the day—
and the following dawn—
when this hat had first
been worn.
Tentatively reaching
(almost too shy—lacking
courage, perhaps—to then
look upon the image to
be reflected), she had taken
and donned
the hat
and saw not
improper nakedness
awkwardly adorned,
but rather a well-dressed spirit,
in proper vestment,
and she had smiled
with warm affection
and knowing recognition
and intimate familiarity
at the reflection
of that
which was real.

Untitled

As I drive lazily northward,
down the darkening highway
that returns to reality,
my mind travels south,
returning to the sultry summer night
of the river city.

With the muggy shadows of the day
shrinking
from the corners of the streets,
we strolled past Romanesque
arches,
offering cordial greetings
to an aged priest.

Beneath the green neon,
amidst the broken tiles
and dusty chiantis,
the flames of ancient candles
flickered,
illuminating ageless attractions.

Respectfully held distant
by social conventions,
but amused by the warmth
of a good red wine,
the natural beauty
of the night remained,
bidding adieu until
a later dawn.

Going Home

Before the plane
yet rushes
through the embracing darkness,
the strongest gusts
are found within,
the roaring engines
again companion to
the liberation of my heart
from the restraining bonds
of life apart,
the adrenalin of expectations
free to pulse
with the pace
and speed and strength
of the roars.
Raging anew,
the innocence and vigor
and passion
which best nourish my soul
are again re-born,
leaving me soaring
toward reunion,
smiling—
savoring the expectations—
still in love
with you.

A Glance Exchanged

It was the denouement
of evening,
a casual night occasionally crinkled
by the warming ebbs and flows of
    — comfortable, mutual affections
    — the textures of plates
      well-prepared, savored with care
    — the quiet thrill of new
      bookshelves accompanied
      by warming fire,
      discovered behind
      a curtain of clattering cups
      and exuberant conversations.
Together,
      tucked into a corner,
the steam of hot drinks
      rising between them,
he and she
quietly shared
spring's first raspberries with cream
      (whipped, but of course)
and renewed,
with the exchange
of one unmistakably
significant glance,
the passion of a lifetime
commitment to coupling—
in all its variations.

A Moment

Transported away
from the responsibilities
of competency,
travelling to
melodies of youth,
tunes ever-present but
rarely sung in the company of others,
she embraced expectations
for the evening,
realized at night's end
not by camaraderie or by good conversation,
but in the simple joy
of a well-swung old swing.

Catapulting away from the earth,
shedding the vestments of growing up—
amidst swirling darkness,
enthusiastic applause
and screams of unexpurgated terror—
it was a moment in life
amidst the routines of living.

Gazebo Dance

They danced alone
across scuffed, oaken floorboards,
laid well and tight
against the wear
of lightfooted dreams
and moonlit fantasies,
the warmth
of mutual attraction
cooled slightly
by a waning seaward breeze.
Barely rustling through the palms
which embraced the gazebo,
the wind
lazily, reluctantly
brought to their step
the last music of the night,
notes adrift from the
far beaches
of the cove.

The podium,
left empty of tune
by the devotion
of hourly musicians
to the regularity
of their paychecks
and not the magic
of the night,

stood a solitary witness
to the gentle, quiet two-step
which silently circled amongst
— discarded shoes long since
    kicked to the side
— fading scents of hibiscus petals
    fallen from pinned floral tokens
— empty glasses
    oft-filled with
    the pressed, fermented
    juices with which
    nature seduces
— shadows of wayward
    glances across crowds
    toward greener fields
— echoes of the unrequited affections
    of ambitious suitors
    seeking companionship
    against the emptiness
    of the remaining night.

Not pulled together
by the instinctive
physical cravings
with which
younger dancers
might pace
the progress
of the night,

adorned
by simple golden bands,
each well-worn
but from different lovers,
the couple yet caressed
the dance as one,
comfortable
in each other's rhythm
though still unfamiliar
with the inner sculptings
of each other's heart.

The dance, at first,
had begun
as an awkward thing,
a welcomed respite
from the difficulties
of mimicking
painless, inconsequential
polite conversation.

But each song
became excuse
for developing addiction,

a lyrical blanket
under which to pursue

— the chill down the spine
    of an inadvertent
    warm, smooth breath
— the playful tickle
    of bare toes
    lightly stepped
    one upon another
— the softening embrace
— the abandonment
    of propriety
    for a knowing intimacy
    for which their words
    had been ineffective
    instruments.

With conversation since replaced by

— the eloquent soliloquy
    spoken by the soft kiss
    of lips
    to each knuckle
    of a hand drawn close

— the whimpered affection
of fingers
lingering across
slightly peppered temples
— the rhetorical elegance
with which the dancers
danced,
swept away by the romance
for which only silence
properly harmonizes

the night went on
and the couple's embrace
endured,
accompanied
by quiet songs
from the stars.

On My Mind

On this evening
as darkness embraces
all which surrounds us,
so my arms seek
to entwine, caress
and embrace
all of you—
roughly, with unrestrained
passion,
battling toward a
mutually satisfying
conquest of the
longing ache
within my heart—
to this thought then
turns my mind
as I am left
alone by your departing steps
into the darkness
of the night.

Sunday Stroll

At the edge of the lake,
the season begins.
Shedding the dull coverings
of winter,
people crowd
the shore,
parading into
the wave-jumping wind
their exuberance
for renewal
of life's cycles.
Brightened cheeks
and frosted breaths
belie the wisdom
of indulging in
the first cone
of a midsummer treat,
but the sweet taste
of the cream's richness
overcomes the chill
which shudders
the huddled shoulders
of the aged huckster's
first customers.

And the crocuses,
following the lead
of the crowd,
burst through
the earth

in scattered, undisciplined
celebration and
force their color
into the warmth
of the sun,
their fragrance
dancing upon the breeze
in a graceful minuet
with the pungent aroma
of the first mown grass.

Amidst
— the street players,
— the escorted strollers
   (trailing behind them
   wakes of turned faces,
   all embraced by the
   eternally familiar
   smiles with which we
   greet our innocent
   heirs),
— barking dogs and crying gulls,
— swans and ducks
   gratefully ducking and diving
   for the abundant
   tossed treats
   of Sunday's extra croissants,
— the first couple
   embracing upon the wall
   in oblivious public
   passion,

— old ladies braving
the sun to walk again
accompanied only
by their memories
of earlier excursions
and
— young men
gathered upon the pier
silently, as one,
indulging in the daydreams
which follow behind
each woman of beauty
who passes,

amidst these renewals,
spring arrived this day
at the edge of the lake.

Untitled

Satiated slumber
remains an apparition.
Insufficient rest again
awaits
beyond her expectations
of the coming night
fulfilled anew.

Crayon Sketch

How quickly vivid moments fade—
impressionistic images begin to cloud
sharp clarities of the recent past.
I struggled, in a private time not long ago,
while surrounded by the saloon noises
and disappointments of the night
that allow every bar to be
a personal retreat,
to recall the brilliance and excitement,
to arouse from within
how that one night's magic
with you
had eloquently stroked
the darkness
with hues of thrilling color.
But, confronted with the empty canvas
of liquored imagination,
my palette was inadequate—
the passionate, sensual pigments
with which we painted
having faded,
run together.

Confused, uncertain ebbs of color—
swirled and indistinctive—
could not adequately illustrate:
— the shiver of a misplaced winter wind
— the warmth of salsa, fermented hops
   and inquisitive conversation
— the intimacy of your knee,
   pressed against mine beneath the table
   with knowing intent
— the acquiescing smile of the aging waiter,
   seeing more ahead than I was
   daring to consider
— the gentle swirl of your body,
   comfortable in an old-fashioned two-step,
   flowing as if you belonged
   into the open arms
   of an awkward dancer
— the stroll down a corridor
   to a well-known rhythm,
   a pace for considering
   whether those behind
   the passing, numbered doors
   have, that night, walked
   a similar path
— the awkwardness of our passion,
   unconsummated in mutual deference
   to social conventions
— the absence of loneliness
   while drifting to slumber
— the reluctance and hollowness
   of the following dawn.

Intent on recalling from our night
a definitive composition,
a reconciliation
of the exquisite, precise,
      sensuous passage of our pleasures,
I found details grown more blurred,
     my palette muddled, deserving
     to be discarded.

With what then was I left to illustrate?
What tools of art were proper to
memorialize the remaining images,
before they too faded, swirled
together and became inadequate?
Looking past the ambered neck
of my evening companion, I saw
next to the well-polished edge
of the wooden bar
all that I needed to render
my composition—
a cup
of children's crayons,
set aside for entertainment
and amusement.

Sketched then,
on the inner folds
of an unstained napkin,
were the indistinctive fading images
of our provocative night—

Relegated to translating
all the vibrancy,
all the hues of our time together,
into the primary colors
of pre-formed waxes,
ably to only pull
the crayons clumsily
across the fragile tissue,
I could draw but
stick-like caricatures
of the emotions past,
reducing all that I wanted
to remember,
and to dream for
perhaps again,
into a bar-room sketch,
to be cleared away
with the evening's debris.

Snowfall

Trekking through the snow, newfallen.
Winter's sun, low hanging
in now blue sky,
so pointedly sharp
in its brightness—
like a stiletto
well-honed with purpose—
that it pierces through the iris
with which I view the world
to illuminate truths within
that others have seen—
that our dreams
will remain as dreams
and that life will expire
in routine degradation
and without consequence.
Above the crunching
of footsteps in snow very cold,
the well-lit silence of my heart
is deafening.

Bathing

It is the same.

First, hot water
burns
the most delicate flesh,
the pain difficult
to overcome—
a price to pay
for the pleasure
ahead.
And then,
ever so slowly,
one sinks,
leaving burned
that which descends
beneath and is immersed,
consumed by the
searing wetness.
Unable
to grow accustomed
to the penetrating heat,
one's heart accelerates,
pounding to keep pace
with the liquid fire
which surrounds,
sweat upon the brow.
At last,
relaxation comes,

toes, fingers,
arms, legs
afloat, adrift . . .
one's soul finally
let free
of that in which
life had adorned it—
the racing rhythm
of the heart
a solitary sound
which overwhelms,
while body parts
and thoughts
become weightless
and unwind.

So it is
that a bath
is the same
as that
which consumes me
when my eyes
fall upon you.

In the Presence of Ancient Viking Timbers

No place to hide.
Exposed, trembling
in the presence
of ancient Viking timbers.
Expectations for the day
overcome in silent halls
by deafening echoes
carried across the ages:
    — gluttonous chortles of expectant pillage.
    — belligerent screams of primal takings.
    — sobbing whimpers of the surviving raped.
    — rhythmic creakings
        of whip-disciplined oars,
        sweeping against her
        in hissing, swift waves
        the ghostly, brutal visions
        of ultimate submissions.
Captured, dominated
by a tender whisper
stroked across her ear,
her body collapsed,
and her soul succumbed,

to the savagery
of her lust, at last
unlocked
while in the shadows
of ancient corsairs
    — to chortle with expectations
      of primal takings.
    — to stroke away the wetness of
      submissive tears.
    — to be swept away in the cascading
      arousal of the orgasm
      of conquest.

Geneva

In first spring night's wind
at the edge of dreams,
lover's tongues battle
for a solitary drop
of well-aged liqueur,
an elixir released
from chocolate wrapping
melted away by their kiss
upon a balcony
beneath guardian alps.

I-71 N (Version II)

The blacktopped passage
through stripped, harvested fields
brings to view
repeating stands
of fully branched trees, tall,
stripped too by nature's
patterned habit
of dressing and undressing
the earth of its bounties.
The endless, greyed
clouds seem
to again and again
stress and shatter against
the branches,
fracturing the desolation
of the day,
leaving room
for travelling recollections.

Untitled

Among dawn's chirpings,
summer's light
uncovers dreams,
first kisses
alive upon lips,
quivering,
still wet
from tears
shed in farewell.

Hammock

Still.
In orange-yellow hues
of reflected morning light,
ropes grayed by exposure,
time's passage and
repeated summer showers,
stretched and sagging
from the playing
and lazing often
hosted elegantly
beneath the full-branched
canopies of oak,
the hammock is now
visited only by
a few well-colored leaves
falling,
caught for awhile
upon its weaving—
like youth's memories,
their color changes too
with time—
the leaves
eventually to fall
again,

leaving the hammock
to meet
winter's approach
alone,
strung above
the decayed remains
of summer's leaves,
an awkward sentinel
guarding the memories.

Escape

As a woman in passion
releases joyful tears,
wetting her cheeks
in abandon,
so do the droplets
cascade
from emerald strands
wistfully overflowing
the fountain's
well-crafted bowls,
leaving concentric shimmerings
among the lazy lily pads
in the couple's
private courtyard.

Sunday

From my dreams I awake
to patterings of raindrops,
symphonic companions
in my solitude
to an awaiting rose,
each petal
to be a kiss
upon those corners
of your soul
untouched
by passion's sculpting,
awaiting, awaiting
for more.

Tabard Virgin

Aching is the weight
of troubles and turmoil,
dragging is the spirit
battled by ancient
companions, both
imagined and real.
Rest thyself
in this inn
of refuge,
away from
communications
and dialogue.
Alone in the company
of a quiet courtyard,
secluded settees
and a silent fireplace,
lips tingled
by sipped brandy,
rest thine head
upon a pillow
of dreams,
align your passion
with the prospects
for the morrow
and the morrow
again beyond—

Go sleep, cherished friend,
sleep.
And in your sleep
fly above
and cry
and laugh
and embrace your
next dawn
in a twirling
Hollywood dance,
triumphing.

Paris Poppies

At an anonymous
country cross-road,
beneath rolling clouds
of departing storms
knelt I,
collapsing into a field
of wild, red poppies,
a blanket
of passion's color
caressing the earth
to the horizon,
each petal cradling
remaining misty drops,
moistened—
    as your lips
    might await
    my kiss—
quivering to embrace
as well
my falling tears.

Get Published, Inc!
Thorofare, NJ 08086
13 January, 2010
BA2010013